W9-BUI-505

Routes of Science

Light

Chris Woodford

BLACKBIRCH®
PRESS

THOMSON
GALE

San Diego • Detroit • New York • San Francisco • Cleveland • New Haven, Conn. • Waterville, Maine • London • Munich

THOMSON

━━━━ ✦ ━━━━ ™

GALE

Every effort has been made to trace the
owners of copyrighted material.

PHOTOGRAPHIC CREDITS
Cover: Pacific Northwest National Laboratory
(l); National Library of Medicine (t); NASA (b).

Corbis: 27r; Archivo Iconografico SA 9r,
Bettmann 33b, Richard Cummins 20, 28,
Roger Ressmeyer 36t; **Getty Images:** Hulton
Archive 35t, 36b; **Image Bank:** 9l; **Mary
Evans Picture Library:** 5, 7c, 7b, 11, 19t, 19b,
23t, 23b; **NASA:** 1, 26, 34; **National Library
of Medicine:** 12, 29c; **Pacific Northwest
National Laboratory:** 25b; **Photodisc:** 4–5,
16, 22; **Topham Picturepoint:** 13bl, 13br,
14, 15t, 15br, 29t, 33t; **Science and Society
Picture Library:** 15bl; **Science Photo Library:**
John Chumack 24r, Jerome Wexler 13t;
University of Pennsylvania: Smith Image
Collection 10, 11b, 24l, 27l, 30.

Consultant: Don Franceschetti, Ph.D.,
Distinguished Service Professor,
Departments of Physics and Chemistry,
The University of Memphis,
Memphis, Tennessee

For The Brown Reference Group plc
Text: Chris Woodford
Project Editor: Sydney Francis
Designer: Elizabeth Healey
Picture Researcher: Helen Simm
Illustrators: Darren Awuah,
 Richard Burgess, and Mark Walker
Managing Editor: Bridget Giles
Art Director: Dave Goodman
Children's Publisher: Anne O'Daly
Production Director: Alastair Gourlay
Editorial Director: Lindsey Lowe

LIBRARY OF CONGRESS CATALOGING-IN-PUBLICATION DATA

Woodford, Chris.
  Light / by Chris Woodford.
    p. cm. — (Routes of science)
  Includes bibliographical references and index.
  ISBN 1-4103-0297-0 (hardback : alk. paper)
  1. Light—Juvenile literature. 2. Radiation—Juvenile literature. I. Title. II. Series.

  QC360.W67 2004
  535—dc21   2003013002

Printed and bound in Singapore
10 9 8 7 6 5 4 3 2 1

CONTENTS

INTRODUCTION

Light fills our world with color and life. Without light, in fact, the world we are used to would not exist at all. Light makes plants grow and provides the foods that animals eat, thus beginning the food chain on Earth. In this way, light makes possible almost all of the life on our planet.

LIGHT IS ALSO INCREASINGLY important to people for other reasons. Modern telecommunications, including telephones and the Internet, rely on beams of laser light that shine through tiny fiber-optic cables. Light makes possible all manner of cutting-edge technology, from telemedicine (in which surgeons use video links to operate on people in other places) to virtual reality, and from special effects in the movies to CD players.

Scientists have spent great amounts of time over the centuries trying to understand light. Although early civilizations knew what light was and how to use it, the ancient Greeks and Romans were the first to try to find out how and why light worked as it did. Later scientists believed that light was a stream of particles, like bullets fired from a gun; others thought it must be a train of waves, like the ones that flow across the sea. Eventually, scientists realized light is a form of radiation similar to radio waves and X rays and that it can be a wave and a particle at the same time.

These discoveries led to the theory of quantum mechanics, which seeks to explain the world inside the atom. Meanwhile, attempts to measure the speed of light produced the world of relativity, where space and time behave in unexpected ways.

The story of light is a tale of how some very different scientific ideas (called theories) gradually build on one another to give us a better understanding of the world. Eventually, through the work of many different scientists and over a long period of time, one theory stands out among all the others as the best explanation of something. In the case of light, that process of understanding has taken more than two thousand years.

1 LIGHT IN THE ANCIENT WORLD

Some scholars believe that the ancient peoples of Mesopotamia, Egypt, and India knew quite a lot about optics (the study of light), although the ancient Greeks were the first to put forward theories of light.

THE EARLIEST KNOWN optical instrument was discovered in 1850 at Nineveh, the capital of the ancient Assyrian Empire. It was a (**lens**) about 1.5 inches (4 cm) wide, made of crystal. It dated from sometime before 600 B.C. Archaeologists originally believed it was used for concentrating

Lenses

Convex lenses bulge in the middle; concave lenses have hollowed surfaces. A convex lens bends light rays from a distant object so they focus (meet) at a single point called the focal point. A concave lens spreads out the light rays. Convex lenses make objects appear larger (right, top), and concave lenses make objects appear smaller (right, bottom). It is the lens in each of our eyes that makes it possible to see things clearly. Binoculars and telescopes use more powerful lenses.

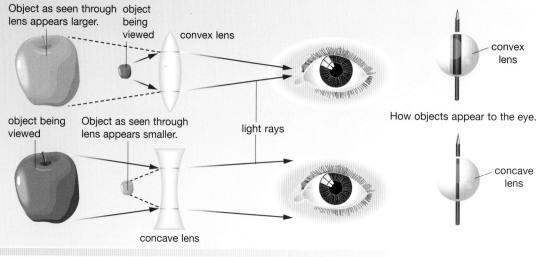

Object as seen through lens appears larger.
object being viewed
convex lens
object being viewed
Object as seen through lens appears smaller.
light rays
concave lens
convex lens
How objects appear to the eye.
concave lens

Reflection and Refraction

A ball kicked toward a wall at an angle will bounce off in the other direction at the same angle. Light rays behave in the same way when they bounce off mirrors or shiny surfaces. This is called the law of reflection (below, left). When light rays enter a denser material than air, they slow down and bend slightly. (Density is a measure of how much matter something contains.) This process, called refraction, explains why lenses bend light (below, right). Refraction is what makes a stick look crooked when it stands half in and half out of water (*see* page 13).

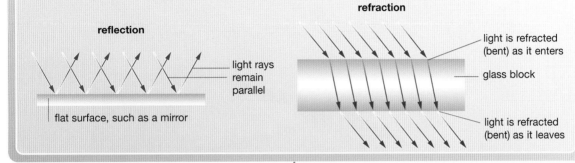

refraction

reflection

light rays remain parallel

flat surface, such as a mirror

light is refracted (bent) as it enters

glass block

light is refracted (bent) as it leaves

the Sun's rays to make fire. Some scholars today think it may have been an early telescope.

The ancient Greeks understood that light normally travels in straight lines. They also knew about reflection and **refraction**. Around 400 B.C., comic

Greek playwright Aristophanes (448–385 B.C.) mentioned the use of lenses to create fire in his play *The Clouds*. About a hundred years later, Greek mathematician **Euclid** wrote one of the first scientific studies of optics.

Euclid's Optics

Euclid (*c.* 300 B.C.; right) is best known for inventing geometry. He used geometry to figure out some important ideas about light, which he wrote about in his book *Optics*. He explained, for example, that light travels in straight lines and that nearer objects appear larger than those that are farther away. In later books, he set out theories of reflection and refraction.

Vision

We can see objects because light reflects off them and into our eyes. At the back of each eye is a collection of sensitive cells called the retina. This contains a mixture of rod cells, which detect brightness, and cone cells, which detect colors. The retina feeds the signals it detects to our brains, where they are turned into the pictures of the world that we see.

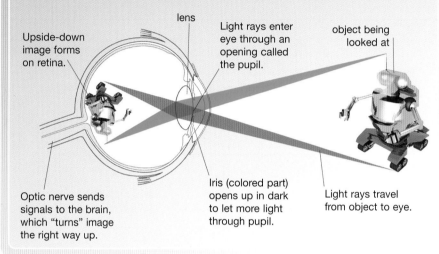

Upside-down image forms on retina.

lens

Light rays enter eye through an opening called the pupil.

object being looked at

Optic nerve sends signals to the brain, which "turns" image the right way up.

Iris (colored part) opens up in dark to let more light through pupil.

Light rays travel from object to eye.

In addition to theories about light, the ancient Greeks also put forward ideas about (**vision**)—how light allows people to see things. In the sixth century B.C., Greek mathematician Pythagoras (*c.* 569–*c.* 475 B.C.) suggested that the sense of sight works in a similar way to how a candle lights a room: we see things because rays shoot out from our eyes and hit objects in the world, making them visible.

Around two hundred years later, Greek philosopher (thinker) (**Empedocles**) argued that we see things when minute particles given off by objects pass into our eyes. He also thought that colors were somehow recognized inside our heads. The idea that we see things because light reflects off objects and into our eyes was first put forward by Greek philosopher Epicurus about 300 B.C.

Although the Greeks were good at coming up with theories, their ideas were often based on their imagination because they did not have the technology to test the theories. Does light travel out from objects and into our eyes, as Empedocles believed? Or does vision work in the opposite direction, as Pythagoras suggested? The Greeks had no way to determine which of these theories was right.

The Pleasure of Epicurus

Greek philosopher Epicurus (341–270 B.C.; below) was born on the island of Samos. He taught his pupils that being happy and enjoying things should be the main goals of life.

Empedocles' World

Like many other Greek thinkers, Empedocles (493–433 B.C.) developed a complete theory of the world. He thought everything depended on how the two forces of love and hate acted on the four elements of earth, air, fire (below), and water.

Testing Theories

A good scientific theory is one that makes predictions that can be tested. Although theories can be proved wrong, they can never be proved right. A new piece of evidence might be discovered at any time that proves a seemingly correct theory was wrong after all.

2 FROM ALHAZEN TO THE TELESCOPE

Scientists finally began to understand the nature of light at the end of the first millennium, when the Arabian physicist Alhazen argued that light travels from the world into our eyes. Later, practical scientists such as Galileo and Leeuwenhoek developed the first telescopes and microscopes.

MORE THAN A THOUSAND YEARS after the Greeks, the debate about how light works was settled, largely thanks to **Alhazen.** In his influential book *Optica Thesaurus* (Optical Treasury), Alhazen rejected the idea that light

Doctor Mirabilis

A great scholar of the thirteenth century, Roger Bacon (*c.* 1214–1294; below) was known as Doctor Mirabilis, which means "brilliant teacher," because he knew about so many different things. His *Opus Major* (Greatest Work) was an astonishing encyclopedia of science, mathematics, philosophy, and language. Bacon was one of the first people to believe in the importance of careful scientific experiments.

Alhazen's *Optica*

Born in Basra in modern Iraq, Alhazen (*c.* A.D. 965–1039) was a mathematician and physicist who published important ideas on geometry and astronomy, although he is remembered mostly for his work on optics. His *Optica Thesaurus* contained theories of reflection, refraction, lenses, mirrors, binocular (two-eyed) vision, and also investigated the workings of the human eye.

Who Invented the Telescope?

Dutch eyeglass-maker Hans Lippershey (1570–c. 1619; right) is generally credited with inventing the telescope—or "looker," as he called it—but some scholars believe telescopes were invented much earlier. More than fifteen hundred years before Lippershey, the Roman emperor Nero (A.D. 37–68) is believed to have used a lens made of emerald to watch a battle from a safe distance. The Nineveh rock crystal (*see* page 6) might be an even older form of telescope.

travels out from the eyes. This was a real scientific breakthrough. It showed that light was something that existed in the world by itself and not something that was created by people's eyes.

When Alhazen's book was translated into Latin in the thirteenth century, his ideas soon began to influence European scientists, including English philosopher **Roger Bacon.** Bacon was one of the first people to suggest that cut-and-polished lenses might be used to improve a person's sight. This led to the rapid development of eyeglasses and **telescopes** in Europe in the centuries that followed.

Galileo's Observations

Galileo Galilei (1564–1642; below) made many important observations with his telescopes. They included the satellites of Jupiter, sunspots, the phases (appearances) of Venus, the gradually changing appearance of Saturn, and craters and mountains on the Moon.

The development of telescopes led to a wave of astronomical discoveries. Within a year of hearing about Lippershey's telescope, Italian physicist Galileo Galilei had built one of his own that could magnify three times. He rapidly improved it so it could magnify twenty to thirty times, and soon began to make important observations of the skies. Galileo also turned his telescopes into microscopes, although the real pioneer of microscopes was Dutchman Antoni van Leeuwenhoek.

Many early optical instruments were developed by trial and error,

Law of Refraction

Different materials bend light by different amounts, but any one material always bends light by the same amount. This is known as Snell's law, or the law of refraction. Using a simple mathematical formula, Snell's law shows how the angle at which a light ray enters a material is linked to the angle at which it leaves. This link is identified by a number called the refractive index.

but that began to change early in the seventeenth century. In 1621, Dutch physicist and mathematician Willebrord Snell (1591–1626) figured out a mathematical law of (refraction. This made it possible to calculate how to make lenses of different strengths that would magnify things by greater or lesser amounts. French mathematician Pierre de Fermat (1601–1665) later showed how Snell's law could be explained by the way light rays slow down when they enter materials such as glass.

Leeuwenhoek Sees Life

Self-taught scientist Antoni van Leeuwenhoek (1632–1723; right) made microscope lenses that could magnify up to three hundred times. With these powerful microscopes, he studied living organisms, including bacteria, and described red blood cells and capillaries (small blood vessels). Leeuwenhoek was also the first person to observe insect eggs hatching.

One of Leeuwenhoek's microscopes (left) that he used to study living organisms.

3 CORPUSCLES AND COLORS

In the seventeenth century, Isaac Newton suggested light was a beam of "corpuscles" (particles). Newton was also the first person to realize that white light was really made up of many different colors.

FROM ANCIENT GREEKS SUCH AS Pythagoras to Europeans such as Snell, generations of scientists had gradually shown how light behaved. Yet no one had managed to figure out what light actually was. The first person to think about this problem was English physicist and mathematician **Isaac Newton** (1643–1727).

One of the greatest scientists of all time, Newton revolutionized physics, mathematics, and astronomy

Newton and the Plague

In the middle of the seventeenth century, the English capital, London, suffered an epidemic of plague that killed around seventy thousand people—nearly a fifth of the city's population. During this time, nearby Cambridge University, where Newton studied, was closed down to stop the disease from spreading. Newton moved back to his home in Lincolnshire (left) for eighteen months. It was a very creative period for Newton: He developed all his important ideas on gravity, light, and mathematics during that time.

by showing how the complex world could be explained with simple laws. He ignored a great deal of existing scientific knowledge because he was determined to find out the truth for himself.

Newton had long been interested in (**optics**) and soon came to believe that light was made up of tiny particles called (**corpuscles.**) This theory quickly took hold because it could explain many of the ways in which light seemed to behave. That made it a good scientific theory.

Newton's Corpuscular Theory

When Newton thought about the way light travels in straight lines, he came to the conclusion that it must be a stream of particles, which he called "corpuscles." He believed particles of light shot out from objects at very high speeds like the bullets from a gun. If light were a wave, as some people had suggested, Newton thought shadows would have fuzzy edges instead of sharp ones. Newton also explained refraction with his particle theory: Materials such as glass bend light more than air because they have more attraction to the particles of light.

Newton in his study splitting a beam of light into the colors of the spectrum.

Opticks

Newton was always interested in light. At the age of 26, he built the first reflecting telescope, which used mirrors instead of lenses. Later, he used it to view the moons of Jupiter. Newton summed up his life's work on light in his book *Opticks*, published in 1704.

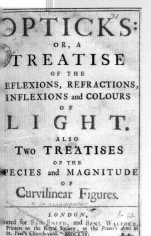

OPTICKS:
OR, A
TREATISE
OF THE
REFLEXIONS, REFRACTIONS,
INFLEXIONS and COLOURS
OF
LIGHT.
ALSO
Two TREATISES
OF THE
SPECIES and MAGNITUDE
OF
Curvilinear Figures.

LONDON,
Printed for Sam. Smith, and Benj. Walford,
Printers to the Royal Society, at the Prince's Arms in
St. Paul's Church-yard. MDCCIV.

The title page from Opticks.

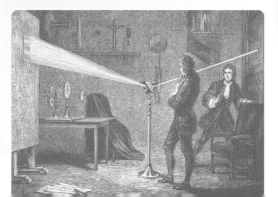

Rainbows

When sunlight shines on droplets of water in the air after rain, both refraction and reflection occur. The colors of sunlight are split as if by a prism and reflected from the back surface of the droplets, so that a rainbow (below) appears in a direction opposite the Sun. Although we usually see only one rainbow, it is possible to see two or more. The less bright rainbows are formed when some droplets reflect the sunlight more than once.

Most people remember Newton not for his particle theory of light but for a quite different discovery. Scientists had known for centuries that when sunlight shone on something like a crystal chandelier, it threw a **rainbow** (spectrum) of different colors onto the wall. Newton, however, turned this observation into a proper scientific experiment. When he shone a beam of white light into a prism (a thick triangle of glass), Newton could see the beam split into a spectrum of different **colors**, which spilled out from the other side. Newton placed a second prism in

Why Things Are Colored

Objects get their color from the light that they reflect. Sunlight is made up of many colors. White objects reflect all colors together and so appear bright and white (**1**). When sunlight falls on a red tomato, the tomato reflects the red part of the sunlight and absorbs all the other colors (**2**). This makes the tomato appear red. Black objects absorb all the colors and reflect very little light, which is why they look so dark (**3**).

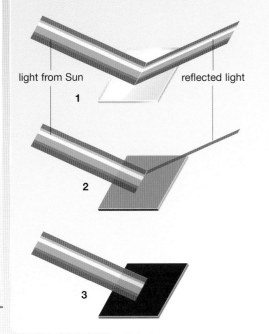

light from Sun   reflected light

1

2

3

Newton's Theory of Color

Newton realized that white light (such as sunlight) is really made up of light rays of many different colors. A glass prism splits white light into colors by bending (refracting) each color by different amounts (right). Violet is bent most, and red is bent least. Newton believed light of different colors was made from particles of different sizes, which traveled at different speeds.

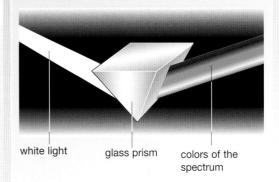

white light   glass prism   colors of the spectrum

the path of the spectrum made by the first prism, and saw that the colors spread even farther apart. He went on to show the opposite result,

too: Lights of different colors could be combined to make white light. These important findings led Newton to his theory of color.

4 | WAVES OF LIGHT

Some of the problems with Newton's theory were solved when Christiaan Huygens suggested light was a stream of waves rather than a beam of particles. Scientists such as Fresnel and Young soon found important evidence for the new wave theory.

ALTHOUGH NEWTON'S PARTICLE theory of light was a major step forward, it could not explain all the different ways in which light behaved. One problem was **polarization**, the way light seemed to dim when it passed through certain crystals. Some scientists thought that light

Polarization

Like waves on the ocean, light waves are transverse waves, meaning they vibrate at right angles to the direction of motion. Unlike water waves, however, the vibration can be either side to side or up and down, and normal light is a mixture of the two. Certain materials absorb light waves with one direction of vibration (polarization) while letting the waves vibrating in the other direction pass. A thin layer of such material is called a polarizing filter. Light that has passed through one polarizing filter will pass freely through a second that has the same orientation in space, but will be completely blocked if the filter is rotated by ninety degrees. Huygens was one of the first to investigate the properties of polarized light.

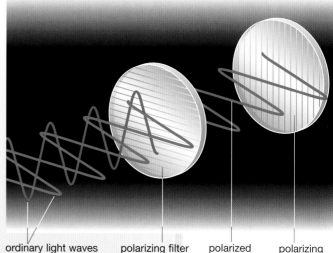

ordinary light waves   polarizing filter   polarized light waves   polarizing filter

could be explained better if they assumed it was a (**wave**) instead of a beam of particles.

The first person to develop a complete wave theory of light was Dutch scientist Christiaan Huygens. Huygens believed that the universe was filled with an invisible substance called the ether and that light traveled through this in the form of waves. Although much less famous today than Newton, Huygens was nevertheless a remarkable scientist who made many important (**discoveries**).

What Are Waves?

A wave of light is much like a wave that travels across the sea. Although the water in the sea is moved about by waves, it is not actually carried all the way from one place to another. Instead, waves carry energy over the sea by moving water back and forth on the surface. Waves are measured by their wavelength (the distance from one crest to the next), their frequency (the number of waves that pass a point each second), and their amplitude (the height of each wave).

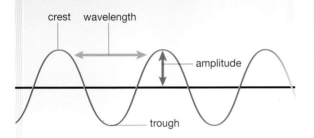

The Great Huygens

Dutch physicist Christiaan Huygens (1629–1695) made the best telescopes of his day and used them to study the rings of Saturn. He discovered Titan, Saturn's biggest moon. He was the first person to make a pendulum clock (below) and later developed the first watch with a spring. Like Newton, he developed important theories of both gravity and optics.

Fresnel in the Lighthouse

Augustin Fresnel (1788–1827) gave the world the Fresnel lens, which is used in virtually every lighthouse and many theater projection systems. Its surface is a series of concentric steps, and each step bends a light beam slightly more. This makes a Fresnel lens much more powerful than an ordinary lens, but very much lighter and easier to manufacture.

A Fresnel lens used in a lighthouse.

Polarization could not be explained by Huygens's wave theory, however. French physicist **Augustin Fresnel** eventually explained the phenomenon by supposing that light was a different type of **wave** than Huygens had originally suggested.

More support for the wave theory came from British physicist **Thomas Young**. By studying the

Types of Waves

Huygens suggested light was a wave like sound that vibrated back and forth in the direction the wave is moving. This is called a compression (or longitudinal) wave, because the wave compresses (squashes) and expands the air as it goes (1). Polarization can be explained, however, only if a light wave moves up and down as it travels forward, like a water wave. This is called a transverse wave (2).

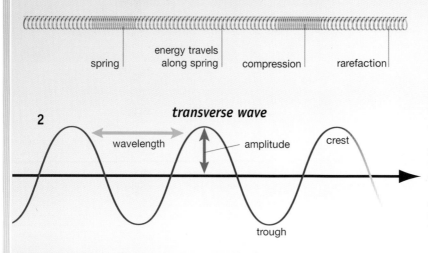

1

compression (or longitudinal) wave

spring | energy travels along spring | compression | rarefaction

2

transverse wave

wavelength — amplitude — crest

trough

1. You can imagine compression waves as energy traveling along a coiled spring. Vibrations occur in the same direction that the wave is traveling. So, energy travels along the spring as waves of compression (squeezing) followed by rarefaction (stretching). Sound waves are compression waves.

2. The vibrations occur at right angles to the direction of movement (black line). Light rays, radio waves, and other electromagnetic radiations are transverse waves (red line).

patterns of (**diffraction and interference**) that were produced when light shone through two small slits, he demonstrated that light was more likely to be a stream of waves than a beam of particles. Separately, Fresnel proved the same result with mathematics.

Although Fresnel and Young offered powerful evidence for the wave theory of light, many people continued to believe that Newton's ideas were right because he was such an important and influential scientist.

Thomas Young

Young (1773–1829) was not only a distinguished physicist, he was also a physician. In 1801, he suggested the first proper theory of how people can see a whole range of colors by sensing only red, green, and blue (below). Young was also interested in the archaeology of Egypt. He helped decipher the ancient Egyptian writing called hieroglyphics on an important tablet known as the Rosetta Stone.

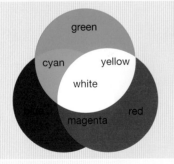

Red, green, and blue light can be combined to produce any color. Blue and green combine to make cyan, red and green make yellow, while blue and red make magenta. A combination of all three colors makes white.

Diffraction and Interference

When light shines through a pair of slits or pinpricks, it spreads out from each one in a semicircle. The spreading effect is termed diffraction. As the spreading beams of light meet one another and overlap, they cancel out in some places and add together in others to make a pattern of light and dark areas. This process is called interference.

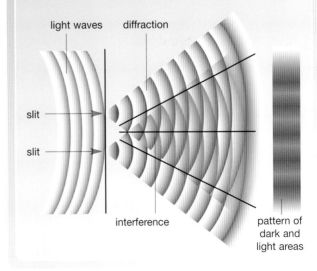

21

THE ATOM BOMB AND THE SPEED OF LIGHT

Many ingenious experiments have been designed to measure the speed of light. These eventually led Albert Einstein to his theory of relativity.

ALL THE SCIENTISTS WHO studied light were fascinated by one thing: the extraordinary speed at which it traveled. Some believed light traveled instantly between two points, which was why **lightning** always appeared

Why Lightning Strikes First

During an electrical storm, we see the flash of lightning (right) before we hear the boom of thunder because the speed of light is almost a million times faster than the speed of sound. Lightning and thunder set out together, but lightning always wins the race!

Galileo's Failure

Galileo thought he could measure the speed of light by timing how long it took to send a flash of light from the top of one hill to another. Unfortunately for this experiment, the speed of light is so great that it travels the distance almost instantaneously. Galileo found out only that it is not possible to measure the speed of light in this way.

Fizeau and Foucault

French physicists Armand Fizeau (1819–1896) and Jean-Bernard-Léon Foucault (1819–1868) made their measurements by shining a beam of light into a piece of apparatus with a rapidly rotating mirror. They figured out how far the light beam traveled as it bounced back and forth and measured the time it took to do this. Then, they divided the distance by the time to find the speed of light.

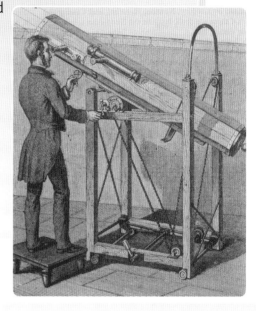

Foucault with a Newtonian telescope he had modified.

before thunder. Others, including Galileo, thought light moved at a fixed speed that could be measured.

The first person to estimate the speed of light was Danish astronomer Olaus Roemer (1644–1710). In 1676, as he watched Jupiter's moons disappear behind the planet, he realized the time it took for them to reappear must be linked to the speed of light, because he would be able to see the moons again only after their light had traveled the enormous distance from Jupiter to Earth.

Accurate measurements of the speed of light were not made for another hundred and seventy years. In the 1850s, physicists Fizeau and Foucault

23

Michelson Measures the Stars

In 1907, German-born Albert Michelson (1852–1931; below) became the first American to win a scientific Nobel Prize. With the interferometer he invented, he  not only measured the speed of light, he went on to calculate the diameter of the star Betelgeuse (right). This was the first time the size of a star had been accurately measured.

The Ether

The ether is not the same thing as the chemical substance that shares its name. In his particle theory of light, Newton had described how corpuscles of light traveled in straight lines through a substance that filled the apparently empty space in the universe. He called this the "luminiferous ether." Huygens also believed in the ether, but thought that it carried waves of light instead of particles of light.

finally measured the speed of light to within 0.06 percent of its true figure. Fizeau and Foucault also found that light traveled faster in air than in water, which was exactly what the wave theory of light predicted.

Fizeau was not interested in simply measuring the speed of light for its own sake. If light traveled through a medium called the ether, as many scientists believed, he thought it should be possible to detect the ether by measuring differences in the speed of light. Fizeau successfully measured the speed of light, but found no sign of the ether.

Shortly afterward, two American physicists, (**Albert Michelson**) and Edward Morley (1838–1923), took up the challenge of trying to prove the existence of the ether. They approached the problem by trying to compare the speed of light measured in two different directions. They reasoned that if there was an ether, light should travel at a different speed in the direction in which Earth rotates than it travels at right angles to that direction. In one sense, the famous (**Michelson-Morley experiment**) was a failure: It did not detect the ether. By the same token, though, it was a great success because it disproved the theory of the ether.

Michelson-Morley Experiment

Michelson invented a device called the interferometer that uses prisms and mirrors to split a beam of light in two. These two beams travel at right angles to one another before they join once again and overlap. If one beam travels slightly faster (or farther) than the other, the two overlapping beams produce a pattern of light and dark areas on a screen by the process of interference. This can be used to make very precise measurements of either the difference in speed of the two beams or the difference in the distance they have traveled.

light and dark areas on screen

mirror 2

beam splitter

diverging lens

mirror 1

laser

The Michelson-Morley experiment proved something else, too: that the (speed of light) was always the same, no matter who measured it or how they did so. This led German-born physicist Albert Einstein (1879–1955) to develop one of the most remarkable scientific ideas ever proposed: the theory of relativity.

Einstein's theory starts from the idea that the speed of light is the same for everyone, whether they are moving or at rest. This leads to a whole new way of thinking about space and time where (extraordinary things) happen to objects that travel anywhere near the speed of light. Relativity also led Einstein to a completely new theory

Speed of Light

When light travels through a vacuum (empty space), its speed is 186,000 miles (300,000 km) per second. Astronomers measure very large distances according to how far light travels in a certain time: A light second is the distance light travels in one second—186,000 miles (300,000 km)—while a light year is the distance it travels in a year—6 million million miles (9.7 million million km).

The two galaxies in this picture are hundreds of thousands of light years wide.

The Effects of Relativity

If a car drove past you at a speed near to the speed of light, it would seem to shrink in size. Time measured on a clock inside the car would seem to pass more slowly than time measured on your own watch. If, however, you measured the speed of light, and the person in the car measured it also, you would both arrive at exactly the same result. These are the extraordinary effects of relativity.

Albert Einstein (below) developed the theory of relativity.

Einstein and the Bomb

Einstein played a key role in the development of the atomic bomb. His theory of relativity proved that tiny amounts of matter could be converted into enormous amounts of energy, which is how an atomic bomb works. During World War II, a group of American physicists persuaded Einstein to write to U.S. president Franklin D. Roosevelt and recommend that atom bombs be made. This led to the development of the first nuclear weapons. Einstein had long campaigned against war and hated the terrible consequences of nuclear bombs that his work led to. He said later, "If only I had known, I would have become a watchmaker."

of gravity, and to the idea that mass and energy are really the same thing. This made possible nuclear energy and the atom bomb.

6 INTO THE QUANTUM WORLD

The discovery of invisible light meant that light was a form of radiation. This important finding led to a revolutionary new picture of the microscopic world known as quantum theory.

ISAAC NEWTON'S EXPERIMENT with the prism (*see* page 17) showed that white light was composed of a spectrum of colors from violet to red. A hundred years later, research by other scientists seemed to suggest that the spectrum extended into other colors that people could not see.

British astronomer William Herschel discovered **infrared radiation,** a type

Herschel Discovers Infrared

William Herschel (1738–1822) discovered infrared radiation when he was measuring the temperature of the different colors of light produced by a glass prism. Herschel moved a thermometer through the spectrum and found that the temperature increased from the violet end to the red end. When he moved the thermometer beyond the red light, he found the temperature continued to increase. This suggested there was an even hotter invisible light beyond the red end of the spectrum: infrared radiation.

A photograph taken using infrared film.

of invisible light just beyond the red end of the spectrum, in 1800. In 1801, German physicist Johann Ritter (1776–1810) and British chemist William Hyde Wollaston showed that there was a kind of invisible light beyond the violet end of the spectrum as well. Known as ultraviolet radiation (or ultraviolet light), this is produced naturally by the Sun.

Scottish physicist James Clerk Maxwell (1831–1879) realized the importance of these discoveries in the middle of the nineteenth century. Maxwell was trying to figure out a theory of electricity and magnetism, known as electromagnetism. He soon realized that a whole range of different kinds of electromagnetic radiation must exist, all of which

William Hyde Wollaston

William Hyde Wollaston (1766–1828; left) worked as a physician until 1800. From then on, he researched many different sciences and made many important discoveries, including the chemical elements palladium and rhodium. Wollaston became rich by figuring out a method for separating platinum from the rocks, or ore, it appears in.

Electromagnetic Radiation

Electromagnetic radiation is produced by electricity and magnetism. Types of electromagnetic radiation include light, infrared radiation, ultraviolet light, radio waves, and X rays. The different types are arranged on a spectrum (right) according to wavelength, starting with the longest wavelengths (radio waves) and moving up to the shortest.

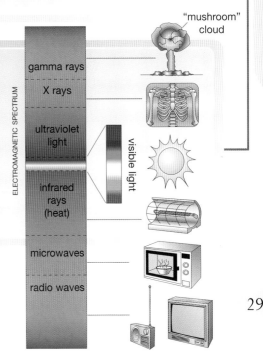

ELECTROMAGNETIC SPECTRUM

gamma rays

X rays

ultraviolet light

visible light

infrared rays (heat)

microwaves

radio waves

"mushroom" cloud

How Electricity and Magnetism Make Light

Electromagnetic radiation travels through space at the speed of light. It consists of two fields, an electric field and a magnetic field. These switch back and forth (oscillate) at right angles to one another and to the direction in which the wave moves.

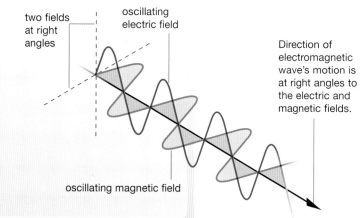

two fields at right angles

oscillating electric field

Direction of electromagnetic wave's motion is at right angles to the electric and magnetic fields.

oscillating magnetic field

Planck and the Nazis

Max Planck (1858–1947; right) won the Nobel Prize for physics in 1918 for his quantum theory. People also admired his integrity and wisdom. In 1937 he tried to persuade Adolf Hitler and the Nazis not to persecute Jewish scientists. This was not his only brush with the Nazis. In 1944 his son Erwin was murdered by the Gestapo (Nazi police) after being accused of plotting to kill Hitler.

seemed to travel at the same speed—the speed of light.

Maxwell saw that light was also a type of wave produced by the combined effect of (electricity and magnetism.) This was a whole new way of looking at light. It was no longer something unique or special; instead, it was simply the type of electromagnetic radiation that people could see. This did not solve the question that had troubled scientists for centuries: What is light? It simply switched that question for a different one: What is electromagnetic radiation?

After Herschel's discovery of infrared radiation, scientists had found that hot objects give off heat by sending out beams of infrared. In 1900, German physicist (**Max Planck**) figured out that infrared could be given off only in fixed-size packets called (**quanta**.) Five years later, Albert Einstein extended Planck's work. With his studies of the (**photoelectric effect**,) Einstein showed that light and other forms of electromagnetic radiation were also bundled up in quantum-size packets. This was the true beginning of quantum theory.

Quantum and Quanta

Planck and Einstein found that electromagnetic radiation comes only in packets of different but fixed sizes, in the same way that laundry detergent sold in stores comes only in certain-size boxes. Each packet of electromagnetic radiation is called a quantum; two or more packets are called quanta.

Photoelectric Effect

When light shines on certain materials, electrons are released. (Electrons are negatively charged particles inside atoms.) Physicists were puzzled by this effect because the energy of the individual electrons did not depend on the brightness of the light but only on the light's color. Einstein solved the puzzle by noting that each electron received a single packet of energy and the energy of the packets depends on the color. This was called the photoelectric effect and provided important evidence for the new quantum theory.

Einstein and the Quantum World

Einstein once said: "I cannot believe that God plays dice with the cosmos." He meant that he found it hard to accept the uncertainty and chance at the heart of quantum theory.

Waves and Particles

Light is normally thought of as a wave, but it can sometimes behave as though it is made up of particles. Similarly, electrons (negatively charged particles inside atoms) and other particles can sometimes behave as though they are waves. This idea, that things can sometimes behave as particles and sometimes as waves, is called wave-particle duality.

Sometimes light behaves as if it were traveling in waves, and sometimes as if it were a stream of particles.

wave

particle (photon)

At the start of the twentieth century, physicists seemed to be no wiser about light than they had been two hundred years earlier when Newton and Huygens had disagreed over the wave and particle theories. Most people assumed light was a wave, but **Einstein's** work suggested, once again, that it was made up of particles (now known as photons). The problem was finally solved in 1923 by French physicist Prince Louis-Victor de Broglie (1892–1987), with the idea of **wave-particle duality**.

The quantum theory revolutionized the small-scale world of atoms and the

Schrödinger's Cat

According to quantum theory, particles can sometimes be waves and waves can be particles. In the quantum world, particles are never precisely anywhere; they have only a chance of being in one place and a chance of being in another. Suppose the same thing applied to the everyday world. According to Austrian physicist Erwin Schrödinger (1887–1961; right), this could have very bizarre results. A cat, for example, could find itself both alive and dead at the same time!

subatomic particles inside atoms just as much as the theory of relativity changed the large-scale world of space and time. The quantum world depends entirely on **uncertainty** and chance and leads to some extraordinary **paradoxes** when its effects are extended into the everyday world.

The Uncertainty Principle

If physicists want to find out where an electron is inside an atom, they can try shining a light on the atom. If light is a beam of particles, though, the particles will collide with the electron, move it about, and make it harder to find. In other words, it is impossible to measure everything precisely in the subatomic world. This is called the uncertainty principle, and it was put forward in 1927 by German physicist Werner Heisenberg (1901–1976; right).

7 INTO THE FUTURE

Although scientists still have much to learn about light, what they have discovered so far has led to important inventions such as lasers, fiber optics, and holography.

USUALLY, LIGHT BEHAVES LIKE a wave. The beam of light from a flashlight, for example, contains many different light waves. All of them travel in different ways, and some of them cancel out the others. If the waves in a light beam can be lined up so the crests of all the waves meet, the result is an extremely precise and powerful (**laser**) beam. Lasers were developed

The Power of Lasers

Suppose all the waves on the surface of the ocean were arranged so their crests and troughs exactly coincided. Waves lined up like this are known as coherent waves. All those ocean waves would add together into a massively powerful tidal wave with huge destructive power. This is effectively what happens to the light waves inside a laser.

Lasers are extremely precise and powerful beams of light.

in the 1960s by American physicist Charles Hard Townes (born 1915). They lie at the heart of many other inventions from CD players to barcode scanners on store checkouts, and from laser-guided weapons of war to sharp and accurate surgical instruments.

Lasers have also driven forward the telecommunications revolution, because lasers are used to send

telephone and internet signals along **fiber-optic** cables. One of the first people to demonstrate the basic idea behind fiber optics was Irish physicist John Tyndall (1820–1893). In 1870 Tyndall showed that light could travel down the spout of water flowing from a can. Fiber-optic cables as we know them today were invented in 1954 by Indian physicist **Narinder Kapany**.

Fiber Optics

Fiber-optic cables (below) are hair-thin strands of glass or plastic that carry light much as electric cables carry electricity. In theory, a single fiber "light pipeline" can carry up to 40 million telephone calls at the same time. The world's first fiber-optic telephone cable was laid in Long Beach, California, in 1977.

Narinder Kapany

Born in northern India, Narinder Kapany first became interested in optics when a teacher told him that light always travels in straight lines. While studying in London, England, in the 1950s, he proved his teacher wrong: He showed that light could follow a curved path by bouncing along the inside of a fiber-optic cable.

How Holograms Work

A hologram is like a three-dimensional photograph made by scanning a laser beam over an object. When an ordinary camera takes a photograph, the film inside records only the brightness of each light wave reflected from the object. Something different happens in a hologram. Normally, all the waves in laser light travel in step, but some of them get out of step with others when they bounce off an object. The hologram records exactly how these out-of-step waves are traveling when they leave the object. When light shines on a hologram, the pattern of light waves leaving the object is perfectly re-created. It is this that makes looking at a hologram almost exactly like looking at the original object.

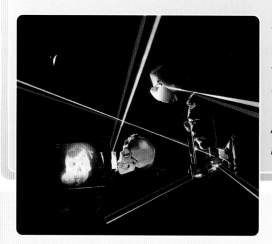

A hologram of a skull is created by reflecting laser beams off mirrors.

The development of powerful lasers in the 1960s made (holograms) practical. Invented by (Dennis Gabor) in 1947, some time before lasers, they are now widely used in many different things, from art and design to anti-counterfeiting devices on credit cards.

Holograms grew out of the scientific theory that light travels in waves. The science of light has spawned a number of other important inventions. For example, Albert Einstein's 1905 discovery of the photoelectric effect provided the basic science behind (solar cells.) The numerous different

Inventing the Future

Hungarian physicist Dennis Gabor (1900–1979; right) firmly believed that inventors should work for the good of society. He once said: "You can't predict the future, but you can invent it."

experiments to measure the speed of light showed that nothing could carry information more quickly between two places. This has prompted the development of ultra-fast (**optical computers**.

The discovery of the electron made the twentieth century an electronic age. With information stored and transmitted by light, computers powered by light, and energy made from light, it seems the twenty-first century may be the age of optics.

Solar Cells

Solar cells work on the idea that light is a particle, not a wave. Each photon (particle) of light carries a certain amount (quantum) of energy. When it strikes the light-sensitive material in a solar cell, this energy is converted into electricity (a flow of electrons).

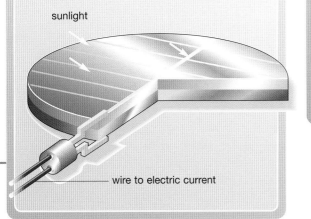

sunlight

wire to electric current

Optical Computers

In an optical computer, information is carried by fast pulses of light instead of slow streams of electrons. Like fiber-optic cables, optical computers can carry many different signals at once. This means they can do lots of different things at the same time (in parallel). Parallel processing, as this is known, will make optical computers much more powerful than electronic computers, which can do one thing at a time (known as serial processing).

Glossary

astronomy The study of space and the universe.

atom The smallest part of an element that can exist. It is made up of protons and neutrons in a nucleus, surrounded by orbiting electrons.

coherent A number of waves whose crests and troughs line up precisely.

corpuscular theory The idea put forward by Isaac Newton that light is made up of "corpuscles" (particles).

diffraction The way light spreads out when it passes through a small opening.

electromagnetic radiation A type of energy produced by electricity and magnetism that travels at the speed of light.

electromagnetism The theory that electricity and magnetism are two parts of the same thing.

electron A tiny negatively charged particle inside an atom that carries electricity.

ether A material that was once believed to fill the empty space in the universe.

fiber-optic cable A thin strand of glass or plastic through which light can travel.

focal point The point at which light rays focus (meet) when they are bent through a lens.

Fresnel lens A powerful lens with a stepped appearance that is used in lighthouses.

hologram A three-dimensional image recorded on glass or plastic with laser light.

infrared A type of invisible electromagnetic radiation that carries heat.

interference The pattern of light and dark formed when two light waves meet.

laser A device that produces coherent light waves.

lens A piece of glass or plastic that brings light waves to a focus by refraction.

light year The distance light travels in a year, about 6 million million miles (9.7 million million km).

mass A quantity of matter.

mirror A polished surface that reflects light waves.

optical Describes an object or process that is connected with light.

particle A tiny piece of matter smaller than an atom.

photoelectric effect The phenomenon in which a beam of light photons causes the ejection of electrons from a metal.

photon A particle of light.

polarization The direction of vibration (of the electric field) of a light wave. Ordinary light is a mixture of waves with different polarizations.

prism A triangular block of a transparent material such as glass, which refracts light into the colors of the rainbow.

quantum A single packet of energy. Two or more packets are called quanta.

quantum theory The idea that energy can be transmitted in packets of fixed sizes, called quanta.

radiation *See* electromagnetic radiation.

reflecting telescope A telescope that uses mirrors instead of lenses.

reflection The way in which light bounces off a surface.

refraction The way in which light bends when it passes from one material to another.

refractive index A measure of the amount by which a material bends light.

relativity A theory based on the idea that the speed of light is the same for everyone, no matter where they are or how they are moving.

spectrum The rainbow of colors formed when light passes through a prism.

subatomic The microscopic world inside atoms.

theory A scientific explanation of something.

ultraviolet A type of invisible electromagnetic radiation produced by the Sun.

uncertainty principle The idea that nothing in the subatomic world can be measured with absolute certainty.

vacuum A completely empty space containing no matter.

wave A side-to-side or up-and-down movement that transmits energy.

wave-particle duality The idea that waves and particles are the same thing.

X ray A type of invisible electromagnetic radiation.

For More Information

BOOKS

David Burnie. *Eyewitness*: *Light*. New York: Dorling Kindersley, 2000.

John Cassidy. *The Explorabook: A Kid's Science Museum in a Book*. Palo Alto, CA: Klutz, 1992.

Gale Christianson. *Isaac Newton: And the Scientific Revolution*. New York: Oxford University Press, 1998.

John Severance. *Einstein: Visionary Scientist*. New York: Houghton Mifflin, 1999.

Patricia Topp. *This Strange Quantum World and You*. Nevada, CA: Blue Dolphin, 1999.

WEBSITES

Lasers—From the Tech Museum of Innovation
www.thetech.org/exhibits_events/online/lasers/mainpage.html
What lasers are and how they work.

The Nobel Prize in Physics—Educational
www.nobel.se/physics/educational/index.html
Information, activities, and fun science games.

Open Directory Project: Light Sites
dmoz.org/Kids_and_Teens/School_Time/Science/Physics/Light_and_Optics
A selection of light sites for children.

Optics for Kids from the Optical Society of America
www.optics4kids.org
Information, activities, and useful links on optics.

Yahooligans websites about light and optics:
www.yahooligans.com/Science_and_Nature/Physical_Sciences/Physics/Light_and_Optics
A selection of websites about light, optics, and color.

Skytopia: Color and Light Trivia
www.skytopia.com/project/light/light.html
Explores extraordinary ideas about light.

Index